IMAGES
of America

SAVANNAH'S
HISTORIC PUBLIC SCHOOLS

Thank you for allowing
me to assist you and
welcome to Savannah!
Dot Owens
7-2007

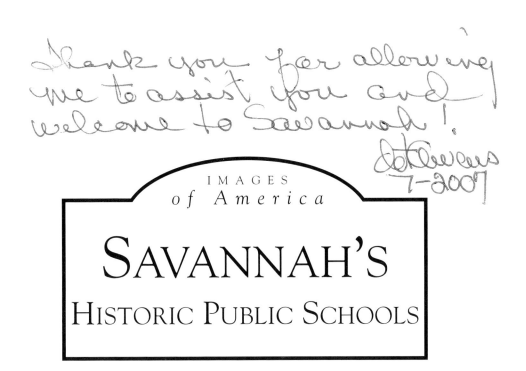

IMAGES
of America

SAVANNAH'S
HISTORIC PUBLIC SCHOOLS

Larry W. Smith

ARCADIA

Published by Arcadia Publishing
Charleston SC, Chicago, Portsmouth NH, San Francisco

Printed in Great Britain

Library of Congress Catalog Card Number: 2004102933

For all general information contact Arcadia Publishing at:
Telephone 843-853-2070
Fax 843-853-0044
E-mail sales@arcadiapublishing.com
For customer service and orders:
Toll-Free 1-888-313-2665

Visit us on the internet at http://www.arcadiapublishing.com

CONTENTS

ACKNOWLEDGMENTS

I have many people to thank for their help with this project. The first and most important is my wife, Lisa Beth. When I was confronted by the intimidating necessity of changing careers in my middle years, Lisa Beth supported our family and put me through school without complaint. She has faithfully supported my every endeavor and is a tower of strength to me. Lisa Beth has helped with every phase of this project from its beginning.

A number of very special friends have lent their advice and talents to this project. I owe special thanks to Mr. Hugh Golson, president of the Board of Education for Savannah-Chatham County Public Schools, and to Mrs. Candy Lowe, administrator of the Massie Heritage Interpretation Center. This book would not have been possible without the documents, photographs, and artifacts they enthusiastically made available to me. Dr. Larry Thompson also provided materials and expertise that were invaluable to this project. The kindness and generosity of these educators is truly appreciated.

Finally, I wish to acknowledge those people who provided the inspiration for this book: the teachers, students, and administrators who have been the heart and soul of Savannah's public schools for nearly 150 years, including, but certainly not limited to, my own teachers; students, teachers, and administrators with whom I have worked; and Gloria, Carolyn, Billy, Ronnie, and Wanda, Savannah-Chatham County Public Schools students of long ago.

INTRODUCTION

As a history teacher, I try to have students grasp two basic historical truths. The first is that we all play a part in the weaving together of human events that constitutes the broad fabric of history; and that as we live, we create an interesting personal history which is uniquely our own. Our sojourns through the educational system are a core component of our personal histories.

Savannah boasts the oldest public school system in the state of Georgia. There are more than 50 schools in the system as of this writing and many more that are long since gone. This book is in no way intended to be a comprehensive history of public education in Savannah; it is instead a look at the city's earliest schools, the evolution of the system, and the experiences of teachers, administrators, and students who attended those schools in the early days of public education in Savannah.

For most of us, memories of school days are among our most cherished. It is a lifelong joy to recall with fondness and appreciation teachers and principals who exerted such profound influences on our lives when we were so very young; and it is equally satisfying to recount the injustices and punishments suffered at the hands of an especially harsh taskmaster. Other school memories include trips to and from school, field trips, athletics and other extracurricular activities, lunches, plays, proms, and especially classmates. Many of us enjoy lifelong friendships that were born in the hallways and classrooms of our schools.

The idea for this book came about when I became the heritage education teacher for Savannah-Chatham County Public Schools in September 2002. Working at the old Massie School, I could not help but be deeply impressed with the rich history of our schools. I am quite literally submerged in this history every day when I go to work.

One day I stumbled upon an old file containing letters written by a teacher named Emma Truslow, who worked in Savannah's public schools a hundred years ago. As I read the letters, I was reminded of an experience I once had while teaching at Southwest Middle School. A seventh-grade student asked me to explain the difference between an educator and a teacher. It was a question of considerable depth coming from a 12-year-old, and I wish I had the letters of Emma Truslow available when I tried to answer, because they provided a profound answer.

Teachers work hard to advance their students. They are patient, kind, hard-working, conscientious, other-centered people. They will discipline students when necessary, but always with a view to improving their charges. Paradoxically they measure their success not by their own advancement but by the successes of others—their students. Educators are very much the same but with an important difference: they perform these same tasks, but as lifelong learners themselves, they also strive to recreate this passion for learning in their students. In my work I am in contact with many teachers of all grades, and I am happy to say that the vast majority of the teachers with whom I have worked are, indeed, educators.

It is my hope that this book will serve two primary purposes. The first is to give readers a historically accurate look at school life in "the good old days" and to provide an opportunity to relive some cherished memories from their early years. The second purpose is to remind educators in Savannah-Chatham County schools of today that they have a long history of success to draw upon. The challenges of today are certainly vastly different from those faced by the educators and students of yesterday, but they can be successfully overcome when met with the "whatever it takes to succeed" spirit that is so much a part of the story of the historic public schools of Savannah.

One

In the Beginning
Massie Common School

Georgia began as a trust colony administered by a board of trustees instead of a royal governor. The trustees provided the fledgling colony with a schoolmaster and supplies. Other educational opportunities for Savannah's children soon became available. In 1788, Chatham Academy was chartered, and it opened in 1813. Chatham Academy charged tuition but shared space with the Savannah Free School, which provided education for indigent children. Pete Massie passed through Savannah as he traveled between Brunswick, Georgia, and Elizabethtown, New Jersey, and he became concerned about the many poor children who thronged the city's streets. When he died in 1841, Massie bequeathed each of the three cities $5,000 "for the education of the children of the poor." Savannah opted to build a school that would be open to all, regardless of wealth. Massie's gift, while generous, was insufficient to pay for the project. The money was invested in railroad and gas company stocks, and in 1855 enough funds had accrued to proceed with the project. Noted architect John Norris built the Massie Common School. The new school was located on Calhoun Square and opened on October 15, 1856. Initial enrollment was 150; the principal and two assistants were supported by another three assistants who functioned in much the same manner as the paraprofessionals of today. By the end of Massie's first year, another 90 students had enrolled. These 240 students, their teachers, assistants, and the school's first principal began a chapter in the educational history of Savannah that would last for more than a century.

MASSIE SCHOOL. This view of Massie School looks south across Calhoun Square. When the school opened in 1856, it consisted solely of the large central building. The western (right) and eastern (left) annexes were added in 1872 and 1886, respectively. Each added two more classrooms for a growing student population. (Massie Heritage Interpretation Center.)

MASSIE SCHOOL. Another view of Massie School, also looking south across Calhoun Square, shows the school's bell tower. The bell was rung by a rope running from the principal's office, located above the building's foyer, through the ceiling and roof to the tower. (Massie Heritage Interpretation Center.)

MASSIE GIRLS' COURTYARD.
This view of Massie looks
northwest across Abercorn Street.
During its first year of operation, a
wall was erected, which enclosed
the "suitable courtyards." Another
wall separated the boys' and girls'
yards and their outhouses, which
were equipped with flushing
toilets. (Massie Heritage
Interpretation Center.)

**GIRLS' COURTYARD, INTERIOR
VIEW.** The girls' courtyard is
shown looking east. The wall at
the rear of the photograph
separated the girls' yard and
outhouse from the boys' yard and
outhouse. (Massie Heritage
Interpretation Center.)

BOYS' YARD. This view of the boys' yard and dividing wall looks west. (Massie Heritage Interpretation Center.)

BOYS' YARD AND THE EASTERN ANNEX. This view was taken from alongside the boys' outhouse and looks north. Originally, the only access to the annexes was through the main building's entrance; note the "catwalk" joining the buildings just behind the metal stairway to the left of the photograph. This stairway provided access to an upstairs classroom that was eventually converted into a library. The corresponding downstairs room eventually became the school's cafeteria. (Massie Heritage Interpretation Center.)

CENTRAL HEATING FURNACE.
When Massie opened, it featured
a central heating system. This
photograph shows the coal-burning
furnace and one of the flues that
conducted the warm air to the
building's second story. (Massie
Heritage Interpretation Center.)

**CENTRAL HEATING FURNACE
CLOSE-UP.** A closer view of the
building's original heating system
shows both flues. During the
Union occupation of Savannah
near the end of the Civil War,
Sherman's soldiers used Massie
School as a hospital. The soldiers
ruined the heating system by
burning wood, including most of
the school's furniture, in the
furnace. When the school
reopened after the war, pot-bellied
stoves in each classroom replaced
the furnace. (Massie Heritage
Interpretation Center.)

FURNACE DOOR. This is a close-up view of the furnace door. The furnace was located in a small basement below the building's foyer. (Massie Heritage Interpretation Center.)

COAL CHUTE. The coal chute for Massie's furnace was located at the front of the building. (Massie Heritage Interpretation Center.)

SINK. Massie School had indoor running water when it opened. The building had several sinks for the convenience of the building's occupants. (Massie Heritage Interpretation Center.)

DESK IN SECOND FLOOR ASSEMBLY ROOM. An old double desk sits in Massie's second floor assembly room. Each floor had an assembly room where recitations—"public examinations"—were held. Note the pine floors and the wooden rails added to the window for the safety of over-inquisitive youngsters. The platform in the background extended around the room and provided seating for observers during examinations. (Massie Heritage Interpretation Center.)

15

MASSIE SCHOOL LOOKING SOUTHEAST ACROSS CALHOUN SQUARE. Massie School's appearance has remained essentially the same since 1886, when the eastern annex was completed. In this view, note that the large original front doors to the main building have been replaced. (Massie Heritage Interpretation Center.)

MASSIE STUDENTS IN 1889. A group of Massie pupils pose for their class photograph in 1889. Compare the front doors in this photograph with those in the previous view of the front of the building. (Massie Heritage Interpretation Center.)

EMMA TRUSLOW. Emma Truslow was born in Marietta, Georgia; her family relocated to Savannah when her father was transferred by the Central of Georgia Railroad. She began as an assistant at Massie in 1902 and was promoted when one of the school's teachers left because of ill health. When noted Savannah educator Saxon Pope Bargeron began researching Massie School's history, she began a correspondence with Emma Truslow Lipps. In her first letter to Mrs. Bargeron, Emma Truslow recalled, "I was at Massie for five years, occupying not only my first classroom, but also the two smaller rooms in the rear of the first floor, and the large room in the center. How did we ever manage? We had no lights in the room and I cannot understand getting through the dark days. And the large classes! One year I enrolled 53 pupils." (Massie Heritage Interpretation Center.)

WESLEY MONUMENTAL METHODIST CHURCH KINDERGARTEN. Before beginning her teaching career, Emma Truslow worked at Wesley Methodist Church's kindergarten. She was later married at Wesley. The church, like Massie School, is located on Calhoun Square. Emma Truslow on the right in the last row. A notation on the back of the photograph credits Wesley Methodist with providing the first free kindergarten in the city. This photograph was taken about 1900. (Georgia Historical Society, Savannah.)

MABEL GOODWIN SAFFOLD. Mabel Goodwin Saffold was at Massie during the time Emma Truslow worked there. In one of her letters to Saxon P. Bargeron, Emma wrote, "Was more than glad to learn of. . . Mable [*sic*] Goodwin Suffold, who took my place at Massie, as assistant when I was given first grade. She was a member of my class in high school, and I always liked and admired her very much." (Massie Heritage Interpretation Center.)

EMMA TRUSLOW'S CLASS IN 1905. Emma Truslow's second-grade class poses on Massie's front steps for a class photograph in 1905. Only 34 students are in this photograph, a very small class for the time. Emma Truslow stands in the doorway. Early in her teaching career she learned that there is always one child who is one step ahead: "I had told my first grade of the two frogs that fell into a pail of milk, and how one kept kicking until he found himself sitting on a pat of butter, while the other frog drowned. At that, one little boy piped up, 'But, Miss Truslow, a frog can't drown.' I, being quite young, and thinking that I must save face, said that, though he could not drown in water, he might drown in milk. Not too many years ago, I told this to my daughter, who is a biologist, and she said a frog <u>can</u> drown. Period. So can any creature that breathes; and where does that put me? The little boy was smarter than I, and I trust that he forgot the incident, but learned the lesson of perseverance." (Massie Heritage Interpretation Center.)

MASSIE STUDENT BODY IN 1905. In 1905 Peter Massie's descendants requested a photograph of the school. The children dressed up for the occasion and lined the front of the building for the photograph. The school's faculty stands in front of the entrance to the main building. To their right the custodian stands in a doorway that allows access to the basement, where the old furnace was located. The coal chute was located in the sidewalk below the window between the custodian and the faculty. Note the open windows and shutters. (Massie Heritage Interpretation Center.)

MASSIE CLASS IN 1905. This Massie class was also photographed in 1905. The man on the right in the last row is Mr. J.E. Way, the school's principal. For most of Massie's existence, the school's principal taught a class in addition to his administrative duties. (Massie Heritage Interpretation Center.)

Weekly Report of *Robert Robinson* during Month of *May* 1903.

100 or P is PERFECT; 95 to 100 is E, or EXCELLENT; 85 to 95 is G, or GOOD; 75 to 85 is F, or FAIR; below 7 is U, or UNSATISFACTORY. Low mark in Deportment means wasted time and hindrance to others.

WEEK	Times Absent	Times Tardy	Deportment	Writing	Grammar	Composit'n	History	Geography	Arithmetic	Spelling	Reading	PARENT'S SIGNATURE
1			7								E	J. M. Robinson
2			U						P		G	M. Robinson
3		1	7						E		G	Mrs. J. M. Robinson
4												
5												

G. J. ORR, Principal.   *E. A. Truslow* Teacher

ROBBIE ROBERTSON'S REPORT CARD. Despite a lapse of some 70 years, Emma Truslow remembered pupil Robbie Robertson—and his mother—quite well: "This little boy, Robbie Robertson, was the brother of the little girl who took a nap in school every day. His 'marks' are pretty good, except in Deportment, and that was my fault for not keeping him busy. After talking to his mother one day, she wrote me a note, saying she thought I should be able to manage a 'six-year-old boy;' and she was right, I should. That was my first year of teaching and I hadn't learned much myself." This is Robbie's report card, signed by Miss Truslow in 1903. (Massie Heritage Interpretation Center.)

FANNY LAWTON'S PENMANSHIP BOOK, C. 1900. Pupils used penmanship books—such as this one belonging to Fanny Lawton—to practice writing skills at the turn of the last century. (Massie Heritage Interpretation Center.)

FANNY LAWTON'S PENMANSHIP BOOK, c. 1900. Shown is the inside front cover of Fanny Lawton's penmanship workbook. Note the instructions on writing position and the proper grip of the pen. (Massie Heritage Interpretation Center.)

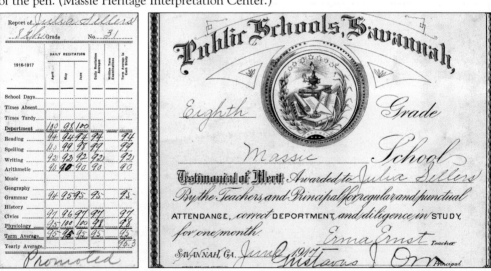

JULIA SELLERS'S REPORT CARD AND MONTHLY CERTIFICATE FROM 1917. Despite large class sizes—sometimes more than 70 pupils—behavior was not usually a problem. Emma Truslow remembered, "Classrooms in those days were usually quite orderly." Good behavior earned the pupil a monthly certificate and, at the end of the term, a certificate for the year. The photograph shows a report card and monthly certificate issued to Julia Sellers in 1917. (Massie Heritage Interpretation Center.)

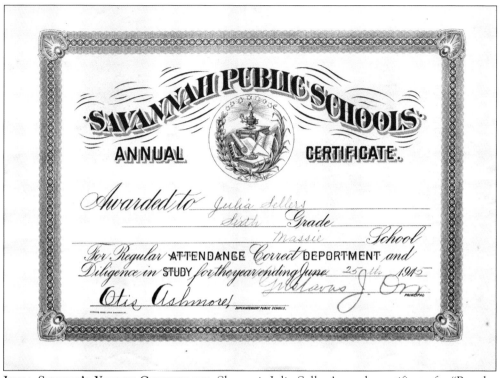

JULIA SELLERS'S YEARLY CERTIFICATE. Shown is Julia Sellers's yearly certificate for "Regular Attendance, Correct Deportment, and Diligent Study." The certificate was awarded in 1915 and was accompanied by a pink ribbon. (Massie Heritage Interpretation Center.)

PAULINE STRADTMAN'S KEEPSAKE BOOKLET FROM 1918. This booklet was given to Pauline Stradtman upon her graduation from Massie School. (Massie Heritage Interpretation Center.)

If all the days that time shall send,
"May "school days" be the happiest you'll ever spend.

Your teacher.
Erma Ernst
Savannah,
Feb. 1. 1918.
Ga

PAULINE STRADTMAN'S KEEPSAKE BOOKLET FROM 1918. The first page of Pauline Stradtman's booklet contained this inscription from her teacher, Erma Ernst. (Massie Heritage Interpretation Center.)

MASSIE IN 1932. The Massie School is shown here as it appeared in 1932. Note the advertisement for White Hardware on the wall of the building behind Massie. In the year this photograph was taken Massie School was inspected by the Georgia Department of Education and scored only 332 of a possible 1,000 points. Major faults were a lack of space, inadequate sanitary facilities, steep winding stairways, and lack of "special rooms." (Georgia Historical Society, Savannah.)

MISS WELLS AND CLASS IN 1946. Miss Charley Wells and her first-grade class are pictured in 1946. One of her pupils, Rosalyn Tillotson, remembered Miss Wells quite well: "I recall my mother bringing me on the first day of school. I was very small of stature and so was Miss Wells and she commented on my size." Miss Wells is on the left of the back row in this photograph. (Massie Heritage Interpretation Center.)

EDYTHE DYSON IN 1946. In May 1857, May Day was first celebrated at Massie Common School. This was the beginning of a much-loved annual community event. Edythe Dyson was crowned Queen of May Day in 1946. (Massie Heritage Interpretation Center.)

MASSIE SIXTH GRADE IN 1946–1947. This photograph shows another of the changes made to the Massie building. The original central heating furnace was abandoned after the Civil War and replaced by pot-bellied stoves. These were in turn replaced by steam radiators; one appears at the left rear of this photograph. The woman in the center of the first row is identified as Alice Arden, principal and sixth-grade teacher during the 1946–1947 school year. (Massie Heritage Interpretation Center.)

26

MAY DAY 1947. Elizabeth All, Queen of May Day 1947, and her court are pictured in Calhoun Square. Wesley Monumental Methodist Church appears in the background of the photograph. (Massie Heritage Interpretation Center.)

MAY DAY 1947. The 1947 May Day Celebration is in progress. Note the city bus in the background. (Massie Heritage Interpretation Center.)

MAY DAY 1947. This is another view of May Day 1947 depicting the queen and her court. (Massie Heritage Interpretation Center.)

A SCHOOL PLAY IN 1947. Massie's assembly rooms had raised platforms where the teachers sat and from which students recited during examinations. The platforms were also a wonderful location for school plays. The photograph shows Massie students performing *Tom Sawyer* in 1947. (Massie Heritage Interpretation Center.)

EASTER 1948. A group of Massie's first-graders posed for this Easter photograph in 1948. The glass panes to the right and left behind the children are built-in shelving used for books and school supplies. The door in the center rear of the photograph led to the principal's office. (Massie Heritage Interpretation Center.)

MAY DAY 1949. The Queen of May Day 1949 was Margaret Ann Westberry. (Massie Heritage Interpretation Center.)

MAY DAY 1949. Linda Johnson and Richard Gormley were participants in the 1949 May Day celebration. (Massie Heritage Interpretation Center.)

MARGARET ANN WESTBERRY, QUEEN OF MAY DAY 1949. In this photograph, Margaret Ann Westberry and an attendant are crossing Gordon Street to enter Calhoun Square and begin the festivities. (Massie Heritage Interpretation Center.)

MARGARET ANN WESTBERRY, QUEEN OF MAY DAY 1949. Margaret Ann Westbury, Queen of May Day 1949, and her court are pictured here. (Massie Heritage Interpretation Center.)

MAY DAY 1950. This May Day celebration at Massie is from 1950. Authors Lee and Emma Adler noted in their 2003 book *Savannah Renaissance* that for a time vehicular traffic was allowed through Savannah's squares located on the streets east and west of Bull Street. A road running through Calhoun Square can be clearly seen in this photograph. (Massie Heritage Interpretation Center.)

MAY DAY 1954. In this photograph of the 1954 May Day celebration, the Queen of May Day and her court watch from an elevated platform as a group of students perform a dance. Note the automobiles parked in the background and the chain-link fence around the section of Calhoun Square nearest to Massie School. This served as Massie's playground; the fence helped prevent students from straying into Abercorn Street. (Massie Heritage Interpretation Center.)

MAY DAY. In this undated photograph of a May Day celebration in Calhoun Square, the photographer has captured an automobile as it travels through the square. (Massie Heritage Interpretation Center.)

GEORGIA DAY. Students dressed in Georgia Day costumes pose on the boys' stairway in Massie School. They are identified as Ronald Hodges, Joseph Gannam, Deborah Mitchell, Christine Easterling, and Lynn Mitchell. (Massie Heritage Interpretation Center.)

SCHOOL PLAY. The student in this photograph is identified as Richard Gormany. The set is located on the stage in Massie's second-floor assembly room. (Massie Heritage Interpretation Center.)

SCHOOL PLAY. The student in this photograph is not identified but is obviously playing a role in the same play as Richard Gormany. (Massie Heritage Interpretation Center.)

SCHOOL PLAY. A group of Mrs. Eloise Rogers's students are shown in costume for a play *c.* 1962. Note the drinking fountain just inside the front door. (Massie Heritage Interpretation Center.)

MASSIE IN 1969. This photograph of Massie School was taken in 1969; the school closed a few years later. The building shows another of the few significant changes in its appearance over the course of its 118 years of use as a public school; note that the breezeways connecting the annexes to the main building have been enclosed. Although Massie School would never open its doors on another new school year, its closing would not mean the end of its service to Savannah. (Georgia Historical Society, Savannah.)

Two

SAVANNAH'S OTHER SYSTEM
EARLY AFRICAN-AMERICAN SCHOOLS

In 1832, a young woman named Emily Burke came south to teach at Bethesda Orphanage. She described Savannah in great detail in her book Pleasure and Pain, *and as a Northerner was very interested in the condition of the slaves. Strict laws forbade teaching slaves to read and write, but many slave children learned through their play with white children. Older slaves were taught by their masters—a slave who could read, write, and do simple arithmetic was a great convenience. After Sherman occupied the city the Savannah Educational Society was created to provide educational opportunities for African Americans, and the Freedmen's Bureau assumed educational responsibilities in 1865. Alfred Ely Beach, a New Yorker, bought a lot on Savannah's east side for an African-American school constructed by the Freedmen's Bureau that opened in 1867. The Beach Institute, supported by the American Missionary Alliance, charged students $1 per quarter. Enrollment soon reached 600. The school came under control of the Board of Public Education in 1867. After a severe fire in 1878 the American Missionary Alliance moved to resume control. The Beach Institute closed in 1919 because of low enrollment. West Broad Street Elementary School opened in 1876 in the William Scarborough House, one of Savannah's grandest antebellum mansions. Despite overcrowding, under-funding, and the challenge of operating in a single-family residence, West Broad Street School served Savannah for 100 years. As Savannah's African-American population grew better schools would come, but many challenges lay ahead in the long and difficult struggle for educational equality.*

West Broad Street Elementary School. In 1876, 10 years after the creation of the Savannah-Chatham County Public Schools, West Broad Elementary School opened to the city's African-American children. Massie School had opened 10 years before the system's creation; records indicate that the delay in opening an elementary school for African Americans was due to the lack of financial support by the state. The school was located in the William Scarborough House, one of Savannah's most beautiful antebellum mansions. Although the house was commodious, by comparison, it was a terribly overcrowded school; at times, enrollment would approach 1,000 students. Massie School housed just above 400 students at peak enrollment. In a 1948 report, West Broad Elementary School was described as "a fire trap." (Historic Savannah Foundation.)

Miss J. H. BROWN . . . . Fourth Grade (B).
Mrs. M. E. TOLBERT . . . . Third Grade (A).
Miss S. C. HOUSTOUN . . . . Third Grade (B).
Miss E. L. JACKSON . . . . Third Grade (C).
Miss L. L. MAXWELL . . . . Second Grade (A).
Miss R. E. LOW . . . . Second Grade (B).
Miss LIZZIE GLENN . . . . Second Grade (C).
Miss R. L. ERWIN . . . . First Grade (A).
Miss CHARLOTTE SPAULDING . . . . First Grade (B).
Mrs. L. A. JACKSON . . . . Assistant.

WEST BROAD STREET SCHOOL (Colored).

(WEST BROAD AND PINE STREETS.)

J. H. C. BUTLER (Principal) . . . . . Seventh Grade.
Mrs. S. J. BUTLER . . . . Sixth Grade.
Miss A. B. MILLER . . . . Fifth Grade (A).
Miss R. A. WALTON . . . . Fifth Grade (B).
Mrs. E. P. DEVEUX . . . . Fourth Grade (A).
Mrs. F. S. MERCHISON . . . . Fourth Grade (B).
Miss G. A. KNOX . . . . Fourth Grade (C).
Miss F. M. JACKSON . . . . Fourth Grade (D).
Miss L. L. CAREY . . . . Third Grade (A).
Miss A. E. SCOTT . . . . Third Grade (B).
Miss A. M. ELLIS . . . . Second Grade (A).
Miss C. E. LEWIS . . . . Second Grade (B).
Miss M. T. B. ELLIS . . . . First Grade (A).
Miss F. H. HOUSTON . . . . First Grade (B).
Miss E. A. QUINNEY . . . . Assistant.

COUNTRY SCHOOLS (White).

Mrs. R. L. GOULD . . . . Bethel.
J. A. METTE (Principal) . . . . Bethesda.
FREDERICK OBORN (Assistant) . . . . Bethesda.
Miss C. L. FERGUSON (Assistant) . . Bethesda.
Mrs. G. H. MILLER . . . . Bloomingdale.
Miss LUCILLE BLOIS . . . . Isle of Hope.
Miss B. N. HOOK . . . . Monteith.
C. H. FERGUSON . . . . Pine Forest.
W. H. BOURNE (Principal) . . . . . . Pooler.
Miss S. C. DASHER (Assistant) . . . . Pooler.
Miss J. C. FURSE (Assistant) . . . . . Pooler.
Miss EMMA HUNTER . . . . South Newington.
T. E. BOURQUIN . . . . Springhill.
Miss A. J. GRAY . . . . Thunderbolt.
Miss L. E. HOLMES . . . . White Bluff.

COUNTRY SCHOOLS (Colored).

Miss G. O. ARTSON . . . . Antioch.
Miss ROSA ASHTON . . . . Beaulieu.
SILAS DANIELS . . . . Belmont.
Mrs. E. E. SPENCER . . . . Dittsmersville.
Miss R. L. BROWN . . . . East Savannah.
Miss SARAH ADAMS . . . . Grove Hill.
S. J. REID . . . . Monteith.
Mrs. F. C. FORD . . . . Mount Zion.
Mrs. G. A. NOBLE . . . . Nicolsonville.
Miss LIZZIE HENDRICKSON . . . . . Pooler.
Miss CATHARINE J. STEELE . . . . . Rice Hope.
Mrs. L. A. WOODARD . . . . Rose Dhu.
Miss ELLEN HICKS . . . . Isle of Hope.
Miss FLORENCE A. LEWIS . . . . . Sackville.
Miss ANNA CARSON . . . . Skidaway.
Miss M. E. BURNS . . . . Taylor's Chapel.
Miss A. B. DeLYON . . . . Thunderbolt.
H. E. BARNETT . . . . Vallambrosa.
Miss ANNA A. BLAIR . . . . Wheathill.
Mrs. M. L. REYNOLDS . . . . White Bluff.
S. M. CHARLTON . . . . Woodstock.
Miss R. E. HARRIS . . . . Woodville.
JOSEPH BUTLER . . . . West Savannah.

Miss N. R. Scott

OLD SCHOOL REPORTS. The Annual Report of the Savannah-Chatham County Public Schools for 1893 is shown here. Miss E.A. Quinney is listed as assistant at West Broad Elementary School. Assistants functioned in much the same capacity as the paraprofessionals of today. Miss Quinney eventually became a teacher; when Florance Street School opened in 1929, she became the school's first principal. She served in that capacity until 1947, completing more than a half-century of service to the public schools and Savannah's African-American community. (Massie Heritage Interpretation Center.)

EAST BROAD STREET SCHOOL IN 1897. The East Broad Street Elementary School's fifth grade poses for a class photograph. (Georgia Historical Society, Savannah.)

EAST SIDE KINDERGARTEN IN 1932. Emma Truslow remembered, "There were no kindergartens in Savannah in those days, except, perhaps, a few conducted by young ladies in their homes, so we started from scratch." As seen in this photograph of a white kindergarten, opportunity was much more limited for the children of the city's African-American community; this photograph shows pupils of the East Side Kindergarten in 1932. (Georgia Historical Society, Savannah.)

MADAME CARGO'S BEAUTY SCHOOL. Some African Americans sought other forms of education. Madame Cargo operated a finishing school for young African-American women. She was photographed (far left, front row) with her 1937 graduates. (Georgia Historical Society, Savannah.)

CUYLER STREET SCHOOL. In 1913, a new secondary school was opened for African Americans. This photograph of Cuyler Street School was taken in 1937. The school would serve adults as well as junior and senior high school students. (Georgia Historical Society, Savannah.)

CUYLER STREET SCHOOL. A class is in session at Cuyler Street School in 1937. In addition to its responsibilities to young African Americans, the school taught literacy skills to adults. African-American women were the unsung heroes of early public education. Few worked in the conditions seen here; they often worked in the most unpleasant of circumstances and were paid less than African-American males, who in turn were paid less than white females. In 1948, average salaries for Savannah-Chatham County Public Schools teachers were: white males, $3,102; white females, $2,169; African-American males, $2,044; and African-American females, $1,964. (Georgia Historical Society, Savannah.)

CUYLER STREET SCHOOL. An adult class is in session at Cuyler Street School. (Georgia Historical Society, Savannah.)

WOODVILLE SCHOOL. Students at the Woodville School created this elaborate display in 1939. The display's title is "Negro Contribution to American Civilization." (Georgia Historical Society, Savannah.)

WOODVILLE SCHOOL KITCHEN. An icebox, gas stove, and a table for preparing food constituted Woodville School's kitchen facility. Note the washing machine in the background. (Georgia Historical Society, Savannah.)

WOODVILLE SCHOOL. Woodville School's young men are shown learning farming techniques. Educational opportunity for African Americans continued to be primarily vocational in nature through much of the 20th century. This photograph was taken in 1939. (Georgia Historical Society, Savannah.)

CUYLER JUNIOR HIGH. A proud group of junior high school students poses for a photograph on the steps of Cuyler Street School in 1940. (Georgia Historical Society, Savannah.)

CUYLER SENIOR HIGH. Cuyler Street School's seniors pose for a graduation photograph in 1940 on the school's steps. (Georgia Historical Society, Savannah.)

CUYLER GRADUATION IN 1940. The Second African Baptist Church was the scene of graduation ceremonies for Cuyler Street School's Class of 1940. The well-attended event demonstrates the support given public education by Savannah's African-American community. (Georgia Historical Society, Savannah.)

HARRIS STREET SCHOOL IN 1941. A class is shown at Harris Street School in 1941. Note the orderliness of the room. (Georgia Historical Society, Savannah.)

EAST BROAD STREET ELEMENTARY SCHOOL IN 1943. This photograph was taken at East Broad Street Elementary School in 1943. Note that the classroom boasts a piano and steam heat. (Georgia Historical Society, Savannah.)

EAST BROAD STREET ELEMENTARY SCHOOL IN 1943. This photograph of East Broad Street Elementary School is also from 1943. Like the classroom in the preceding photograph, the room is well organized and appointed. Georgia, like all states, spent substantially less per student for African-American schools than it did for white schools, but was a leader among Southern states in appropriations for the funding of African-American schools. (Georgia Historical Society, Savannah.)

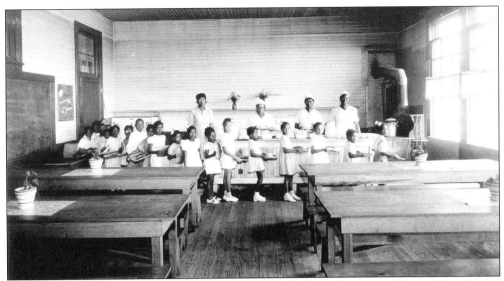

WEST SAVANNAH SCHOOL IN 1944. This photograph shows the serving line and lunchroom of West Savannah School in 1944. Despite the spartan conditions, note the orderliness of the room and the plants placed on each table. (Georgia Historical Society, Savannah.)

MABINETTE KINDERGARTEN IN 1946. A group of pupils pose for a photograph with their teacher at Mabinette Kindergarten in 1946. Note the framed photograph of President Franklin D. Roosevelt in the background. Compare this photograph to the one of East Side Kindergarten on page 40. (Georgia Historical Society, Savannah.)

PRICE STREET SCHOOL IN 1946. African-American schools also celebrated May Day. This photograph shows Price Street School's May Day Queen and court in 1946. (Georgia Historical Society, Savannah.)

PRICE STREET SCHOOL IN 1946. The highlight of the May Day celebration is the Maypole Dance, in which students wind their ribbons around the maypole. This photograph was also taken at Price Street School's 1946 celebration. (Georgia Historical Society, Savannah.)

PAULSEN STREET SCHOOL IN 1946. The faculty and student body of Paulsen Street School posed for this photograph in 1946. This building was originally a factory; architectural drawings for a proposed modern replacement exist, but the project never advanced beyond the planning stage. (Georgia Historical Society, Savannah.)

49

HAVEN HOME SCHOOL IN 1946. This class and its teacher were photographed at Haven Home School in 1946. (Georgia Historical Society, Savannah.)

HAVEN HOME SCHOOL IN 1946. A social function for older students was also photographed at Haven Home School in 1946. (Georgia Historical Society, Savannah.)

HAVEN HOME SCHOOL IN 1946. This is another view of the dinner and dance held at Haven School for the older students in 1946. (Georgia Historical Society, Savannah.)

HARRIS STREET SCHOOL IN 1948. Harris Street School's lunchroom was photographed in 1948. Like West Savannah School's lunchroom in a previous photograph, the room is orderly and each table has a vase with flowers. Note the examples of student work on the walls. (Georgia Historical Society, Savannah.)

HARRIS STREET SCHOOL IN, 1952. In addition to teaching academics, African-American schools also taught citizenship and participation in the democratic process. This photograph shows an elaborate student election at Harris Street School in 1952. (Georgia Historical Society, Savannah.)

SHOP CLASS. In a 1950s photograph, young African-American men learn woodworking techniques in industrial arts ("shop") class. (Massie Heritage Interpretation Center.)

HOME ECONOMICS. In this photograph, also from the 1950s, a panel of judges grades entries in a cooking contest for an African-American girls' home economics class. (Massie Heritage Interpretation Center.)

GRADUATION DAY. Savannah's Municipal Auditorium was packed for this graduation ceremony for African Americans. While the photograph is undated, it appears to have been taken in the 1950s. Once again, enthusiastic support for its schools by the African-American community is clearly demonstrated. One graduate remembered receiving a diploma with "Savannah High School" lined out and his school's name written in. (Massie Heritage Interpretation Center.)

Three

GROWING PAINS

THE SCHOOLS GROW WITH SAVANNAH'S POPULATION

James Edward Oglethorpe's plan for Savannah in 1733 called for a system of wards, each consisting of a central square, four large trust lots, and 40 smaller house lots. Oglethorpe laid out an area of 2.2 square miles for the city; by 1856, 24 wards occupied this space. Early downtown schools such as Massie Common School, Chatham Academy, and Barnard Street School had to function within Savannah's plan. By the turn of the century, transportation had facilitated the growth of suburbs to the south. New schools were needed to serve the area, and they were very different from the downtown schools. Because the city had discontinued Oglethorpe's elegant city plan south of Gaston Street, schools could be larger and more centrally located. The availability of transportation beginning in 1919 meant that students could be safely and efficiently transported to and from the new, larger schools. The consolidation of city and county schools in 1866 meant that the board of education was responsible for all public schools located in Chatham County. Schools had to be built, staffed, and maintained in the smaller municipalities as well as the West Savannah community. The small neighborhood schoolhouses became large educational complexes. Savannah High School best demonstrates the evolution of the schools. Originally meeting at the site of Chatham Academy, the school was relocated in the late 1930s. The new facility could accommodate more than 2,000 students. Today, Savannah High School is located on Pennsylvania Avenue in a new building opened in 1997.

CHATHAM ACADEMY IN 1896. Chatham Academy was chartered in 1788 by the Georgia General Assembly and began operation in the early 19th century. The academy occupied the northeast tithing in Brown Ward, which it shared with the Union Society on the western end of the property on Bull Street. The Union Society rented its portion of the property to the Pavilion Hotel, but eventually made that space available to the Board of Education for an expansion of the school. It was a common practice in the early 20th century to designate sites for specific uses. One year, the first floor of Massie School was the Girls' Grammar School while the second floor was the Girls' Intermediate School; a similar arrangement accommodated the city's boys at Barnard Street School. All high school students, regardless of sex, attended classes at Chatham Academy. At one time, Chatham Academy shared this building with eight separate private schools. (Georgia Historical Society, Savannah.)

HENRY STREET SCHOOL. Henry Street School opened in 1892, becoming the first school located south of what is today the National Landmark Historic District. This photograph was taken in 1962. (Georgia Historical Society, Savannah.)

ANDERSON STREET SCHOOL. At times schools had to improvise to keep pace with the student population of a growing city. Anderson Street School opened in 1896; before its first year of operation was over, the school's second-floor hallway was cordoned off with heavy curtains to create four additional classrooms. This photograph was taken in 1979. (Georgia Historical Society, Savannah.)

CHATHAM HALL. In 1901, Chatham Hall opened on the site of Chatham Academy. The original structure was destroyed in a fire that, according to some sources, was set by a disgruntled student. Chatham Hall eventually became Oglethorpe Avenue Elementary School. This photograph was taken during World War II. (Georgia Historical Society, Savannah.)

SAVANNAH HIGH SCHOOL IN 1905. When Chatham Hall was completed, the building formerly occupied by the Pavilion Hotel was dismantled and a new building erected for high school classes. The old Chatham Academy was memorialized on the building's façade. The school was eventually named Savannah High School, but throughout the 20th century it was universally referred to as "High School," a custom established when all of the city's high school students attended Chatham Academy. After Savannah High School relocated to Washington Avenue in the late 1930s, this building became Chatham Junior High School. (Georgia Historical Society, Savannah.)

RICHARD ARNOLD JUNIOR HIGH SCHOOL IN 1922. Richard Arnold Junior High School opened in 1922. The school was located on Bull Street, well south of Gaston Street. The school was not confined by the space limitations imposed on Savannah High School by the original city plan; compare Richard Arnold to Savannah High School in the previous photograph. In this view, students and faculty pose outside their new modern school building. (Georgia Historical Society, Savannah.)

RICHARD ARNOLD JUNIOR HIGH SCHOOL IN 1922. This photograph is a rear view of the new Richard Arnold Junior High School taken in 1922. There was ample room for students to participate in outdoor activities—until the space was occupied by other buildings. Commercial High School eventually occupied this building jointly with Richard Arnold Junior High School. (Georgia Historical Society, Savannah.)

CHARLES ELLIS ELEMENTARY SCHOOL IN 1931. Charles Ellis Elementary School opened as 48th Street School and was one of the new, larger schools located to the south. It is noteworthy that during the lean years of the Great Depression, Savannah-Chatham County Public Schools not only continued to function, but actually continued to grow. (Georgia Historical Society, Savannah.)

FELL AVENUE SCHOOL IN THE 1930S. This photograph of Fell Avenue School, taken in the 1930s, demonstrates that not all of the newer schools were as grand as the new Richard Arnold and Charles Ellis school buildings. Fell Avenue School had four classrooms and served approximately 180 white students in the West Savannah community. (Georgia Historical Society, Savannah.)

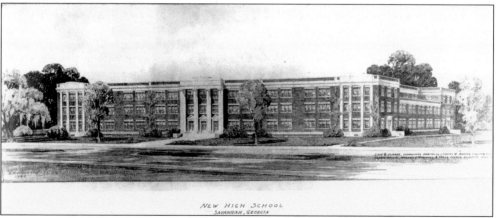

ARCHITECT'S VIEW OF THE NEW SAVANNAH HIGH SCHOOL BUILDING. The continued growth of "High School" meant that more space was needed. The school board already rented an entire building from the neighboring Independent Presbyterian Church to house its Commercial Department, and still more space was needed. A site located in Ardsley Park became available. Originally planned as the Georgia Hotel, where potential buyers of property in the new development could be entertained, the project was abandoned after the foundation was poured because of the Great Depression. (Georgia Historical Society, Savannah.)

SAVANNAH HIGH SCHOOL UNDER CONSTRUCTION. Savannah High School's new building was completed with federal assistance. The Public Works Administration, one of President Franklin D. Roosevelt's New Deal agencies, provided financial assistance to public works projects that followed strict government guidelines. Work was limited to 32 hours per week, African Americans had to be included in the labor force, and as much work as possible was to be done by hand. The new Savannah High School facility was the largest construction project of its time in Georgia. (Georgia Historical Society, Savannah.)

SAVANNAH HIGH SCHOOL AT COMPLETION. This photograph shows Savannah High School's newly completed building. The view is looking southwest. (Georgia Historical Society, Savannah.)

SAVANNAH HIGH SCHOOL IN 1940. This view of Savannah High's band was taken in 1940. Compared to the campus at 208 Bull Street, the school's new location was spacious. (Georgia Historical Society, Savannah.)

Four

School Life
in Savannah

In a school system as old as Savannah-Chatham County Public Schools, there is an unsurpassed richness in the collective memory of people, places, and events. The experience of the schools varied widely depending on the time one attended them. Early Savannah students enjoyed central heating, modern sanitary facilities, and indoor running water. However, students of today are shocked to learn how very different the school experiences of their predecessors in the school system were. As many as 80 students, in three different grades, sometimes shared a single classroom—and a single teacher. Emma Truslow remembered that, because of fire concerns, students worked by the light available through their classroom's windows. There were no gymnasiums, lunchrooms, or libraries. Boys and girls were routinely separated, in some instances entering their school by different entrances. Discipline was strict; good behavior was rewarded by recognition, usually by certificates of merit, and misbehavior often earned the offender a paddling. Students received grades in deportment just as they did in their coursework. Students of yesteryear gave public examinations attended by the public as well as teachers and classmates. Students were expected to demonstrate, beyond the shadow of a doubt, their mastery of subject material before being promoted to the next grade. Teachers and administrators were quick to fail low-achieving students, as statistics in 1871 demonstrate: Promoted (%): Girls' Primary School (Massie) 50/176 (29%); Boys' Intermediate School (Barnard Street) 52/120 (36%); Girls' High School (Chatham Academy) 0/125 (0%); Boys' High School (Chatham Academy 0/90 (0%).

CHATHAM ACADEMY IN 1880. The Girls' High School Class poses with their teacher at Chatham Academy. This photograph was taken in 1880. Note the room number over the door. (Georgia Historical Society, Savannah.)

CHATHAM ACADEMY IN 1882. This photograph, taken in 1882, shows the Boys' High School at Chatham Academy. It was obviously taken in the same location as the preceding photograph. (Georgia Historical Society, Savannah.)

MASSIE SCHOOL AT THE TURN OF THE LAST CENTURY. Massie students pose for the photographer in front of the school's main entrance. Separate entrances were not provided for the two annexes. Students entered through these doors, climbed the stairs, and crossed breezeways to enter the annexes' upper classrooms. Note the slate board with class information between the two girls in the front row. (Massie Heritage Interpretation Center.)

BARNARD STREET SCHOOL IN 1910. Miss Lanneau and her third-grade students pose at Barnard Street School in 1910. First known as "the Public School," the original building was of two-story frame construction. Like Massie, the building was requisitioned by occupying federal forces near the end of the Civil War. For a time, Massie served students living east of Whitaker Street, and Barnard Street School served students living west of Whitaker Street. (Massie Heritage Interpretation Center.)

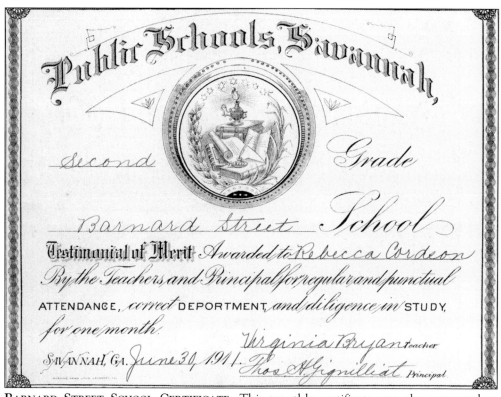

BARNARD STREET SCHOOL CERTIFICATE. This monthly certificate was also presented to Rebecca Cordon in 1911. (Massie Heritage Interpretation Center.)

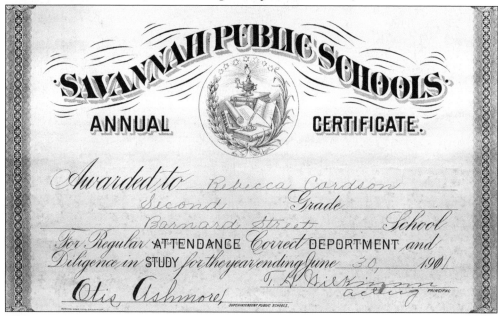

BARNARD STREET SCHOOL CERTIFICATE. This yearly certificate was presented to Rebecca Cordon in 1911. Note that the '0' has been changed to a '1' in the certificate's date. (Massie Heritage Interpretation Center.)

THE SAVANNAH HIGH SCHOOL MONTHLY. A PAPER PUBLISHED BY STUDENTS OF THE S.H.S.

VALENTINE NUMBER

February : : : : 1907

Vol. 2 : FIVE CENTS : No. 1

SAVANNAH HIGH SCHOOL MONTHLY PAPER FROM 1907. Savannah High School was the first high school in Georgia to produce a monthly paper. Teachers contributed articles about such subjects as essay writing and good study habits. (Massie Heritage Interpretation Center.)

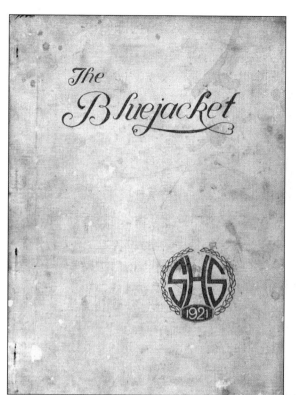

THE *BLUE JACKET* FROM 1921. "High School" students also produced yearbooks. This one is from 1921. The school's mascot, Blue Jacket, originated with boys' blue jackets worn on examination days. (Massie Heritage Interpretation Center.)

THE *BLUE JACKET* FROM 1926. The 1926 edition of the *Blue Jacket* featured a crest on its front cover showing the school's building at 208 Bull Street. (Massie Heritage Interpretation Center.)

THE *BLUE JACKET* FROM 1926.
This photograph of the girls' basketball team is taken from the 1926 *Blue Jacket*. (Massie Heritage Interpretation Center.)

SAVANNAH HIGH SCHOOL DRUM AND BUGLE CORPS IN 1914.
This photograph was taken on the front steps of Independent Presbyterian Church in 1914 and shows the school's Drum and Bugle Corps. (Georgia Historical Society, Savannah.)

SCHOOL BUSES AT THE MUNICIPAL AUDITORIUM IN 1919. In this 1919 photograph, school bus drivers pose with their vehicles in front of Savannah's Municipal Auditorium. The auditorium was razed to make way for a new civic center in the late 1960s. (Georgia Historical Society, Savannah.)

MONTGOMERY STREET DAY NURSERY IN 1931. A nursery school class and teachers stand before their school in 1931. This photograph illustrates well Emma Truslow's comments about kindergartens in the early 20th century. (Georgia Historical Society, Savannah.)

EAST SIDE KINDERGARTEN IN 1932. This photograph of East Side Kindergarten, taken in 1932, has an unusual object in its background: Savannah Gas Company's storage tank. (Georgia Historical Society, Savannah.)

THE SAVANNAH HIGH SCHOOL-BENEDICTINE CADETS FOOTBALL GAME IN 1924. In the absence of other public high schools, Savannah High entered into a rivalry with Benedictine, a Catholic academy for boys. The rivalry lasted for many decades and the annual football game was a much-anticipated community event. In this photograph, one of the players is being tended to in the right foreground. Note the huge crowd. (Georgia Historical Society, Savannah.)

THE SAVANNAH HIGH SCHOOL-BENEDICTINE CADETS FOOTBALL GAME IN 1924. Another view of the 1924 Jackets-Cadets football game shows the players' bench. Note the scoreboard in the background; this view also gives an idea of the size of the crowds attracted to the annual game. Attendance was estimated at 10,000 by Savannah High's coach for the 1926 game between the rival schools. (Georgia Historical Society, Savannah.)

SAVANNAH HIGH SCHOOL AND GLYNN ACADEMY. Savannah High's football team sometimes played practice games with out-of-city teams. This undated photograph was taken during a scrimmage against Brunswick's Glynn Academy. (Georgia Historical Society, Savannah.)

THE PASSENGER LIST OF RMS CEDRIC IN 1930. The passenger list of RMS *Cedric* in 1930 included a number of new graduates from Savannah High School. The graduates toured Europe during July and August and embarked in the vessel for the trip home. (Massie Heritage Interpretation Center.)

ELECTRIC SLIDE PROJECTOR. This projector, from the early 20th century, demonstrates that integrating technology ("InTech" to today's educators) is not a new concept in Savannah–Chatham County Schools. The slides are glass plates, stored in the cabinet's drawers. The projector still works. (Massie Heritage Interpretation Center.)

MICROSCOPE SLIDES FROM 1907. This set of microscope slides is from *c.* 1907. The slides are specimens of various animal and plant cells. (Massie Heritage Interpretation Center.)

DOUBLE SLATE-BOARD AND BOOK STRAP FROM THE 19TH CENTURY. A well-equipped pupil at Massie or Barnard Street School might own a double slate-board or this book-carrying harness that would allow several textbooks to be transported securely. (Massie Heritage Interpretation Center.)

AN EARLY LUNCHBOX. In the years before cigarette smoking became popular, many people chewed tobacco. The R.J. Reynolds Tobacco Company packaged their chewing tobacco in tins such as the one in the photograph. It is clearly intended to be used as a child's lunchbox and is decorated with pictures of George Washington. The tobacco tin is of a similar size as the lunchboxes carried by students today. (Massie Heritage Interpretation Center.)

SAFETY PATROL BADGES. It was a great honor to be selected as a member of a school's safety patrol. The badge on the left was worn in the 1960s on a Sam Brown-type belt. A member of Massie School's safety patrol wore the smaller badge on the right in 1932. (Massie Heritage Interpretation Center.)

48TH STREET ELEMENTARY SCHOOL IN 1931. Students pose with their school buses in front of their new school. This photograph of 48th Street Elementary School was taken in 1931. Savannah-Chatham County Public Schools not only continued to function during the Great Depression, but managed to expand as needed to accommodate the city's student population. (Georgia Historical Society, Savannah.)

48TH STREET ELEMENTARY SCHOOL IN 1931. Students board their buses for the trip home from 48th Street. Safe, efficient transportation allowed newer schools to be larger and more centrally located. Bus duty was added to the list of teachers' responsibilities; note the teacher at the door of the bus on the left. (Georgia Historical Society, Savannah.)

Bus #17 in 1934. Bus #17 is parked in front of the Municipal Auditorium in 1934. Note that the exhaust pipe ends in front of the rear wheels, squarely beneath the passenger compartment. (Georgia Historical Society, Savannah.)

Bus #22 in 1934. Bus #22 was also photographed at the Municipal Auditorium in 1934. (Georgia Historical Society, Savannah.)

Bus #22 in 1934. This side view of bus #22 was also taken at the Municipal Auditorium. (Georgia Historical Society, Savannah.)

Walker Kindergarten in 1939. Most children continued to enter school without attending kindergarten; some were fortunate enough to enjoy the experience. The Walker Kindergarten, photographed in 1939, was well appointed and furnished. (Georgia Historical Society, Savannah.)

SAVANNAH HIGH SCHOOL IN 1940. As political conditions in Europe deteriorated in the late 1930s, the Reserve Officer Training Corps (ROTC) was created. Instructors were retired army non-commissioned officers and they sought to lay the foundation for later, more comprehensive military training if necessity required it. Young men completed two years of the mandatory program. In 1940, Savannah High School's ROTC cadets posed for this photograph. (Georgia Historical Society, Savannah.)

PAPE SCHOOL IN 1940. The growth of the Savannah-Chatham County Public Schools System did not mean the end of private schools. Nina Anderson Pape taught at Massie School before leaving to start her own school. This photograph of her school, located on Forsyth Park, was taken in 1940, and Mrs. Pape appears at the top of the stairs on the right. The Pape School became the nucleus around which Savannah Country Day School was later formed. (Georgia Historical Society, Savannah.)

WESTSIDE SCHOOL IN 1942. As they had throughout all of the trying periods during the nation's history, Savannah's schools continued to serve the city's youth during the World War II years. This photograph, taken in 1942, shows the students of Westside School outside the school building. (Georgia Historical Society, Savannah.)

JOHN VARNEDOE IN 1946. Mr. John Varnedoe was Savannah High School's principal in 1946. (Georgia Historical Society, Savannah.)

MISS ROMANA RILEY. Romana Riley would certainly be numbered among the most remarkable educators who served in the Savannah-Chatham County Public Schools. Born in Augusta on July 14, 1873, her family moved to Savannah when she was very young. She attended Massie School and eventually graduated from Chatham Academy. She became a teacher at Anderson Street School in 1892 and, after 32 years of service, became the principal of Waters Avenue School. Her introduction of progressive educational reform in her school was a great success despite an early period of bitter controversy. (Dr. Larry Thompson.)

WATERS AVENUE SCHOOL IN 1946. Waters Avenue School became "Midget Savannah." The school's organization was modeled after that of the city government of Savannah. Students ran for office, served on committees, and met regularly to discuss progress on meeting the goals set for the school year. One office-holder, suffering a temporary lapse of judgment, came to school armed with a slingshot. When he shot a bird on the school's playground, he was promptly impeached and removed from office. The photograph above shows Midget Savannah's officers for 1946. (Georgia Historical Society, Savannah.)

THE NEWS REEL FROM JUNE 1928. Once Waters Avenue School had organized Midget Savannah, a means was needed to apprise citizens of events and schools news. The school is believed to have been the first elementary school in Georgia to publish a newspaper; the photograph shows the June, 1928 edition. (Dr. Larry Thompson.)

WATERS AVENUE SCHOOL IN 1946. Progressive educational reform called for a radical change in classroom procedures. Teachers at Waters Avenue School coached their students as they completed group activities combining elements from several subject areas. In this 1946 photograph the teacher, at center background, works with one group while other groups complete assignments and enjoy reading. (Georgia Historical Society, Savannah.)

WATERS AVENUE SCHOOL IN 1946. This is another view of students at work 1946. While one group rehearses a play, another completes assignments at a nearby table. Despite sometimes-heated resistance to Romana Riley's methods, her reform of Waters Avenue School was very successful. Educators from other cities often traveled to Savannah to visit and observe the school in operation. When Romana Riley retired, a group of citizens successfully petitioned the board of education to rename the school in her honor. (Georgia Historical Society, Savannah.)

WATERS AVENUE SCHOOL IN 1946. This photograph shows Waters Avenue School students about to enjoy lunch in the school's basement lunchroom. Volunteering mothers of school students often assisted the lunchroom staff. (Georgia Historical Society, Savannah.)

WATERS AVENUE SCHOOL IN 1946. The lunchroom staff is shown preparing a meal in the school's kitchen. Lunchroom staff in the old schools had to contend with steam pipes that ran from boilers located in the basement to radiators in the classrooms above. (Georgia Historical Society, Savannah.)

COMMERCIAL HIGH SCHOOL IN 1948. In 1932, Savannah High School's Commercial Department rented space from the Independent Presbyterian Church. Fully one-third of Savannah High School's enrollment belonged to the Commercial Department. When Savannah High moved to its new building on Washington Avenue in 1937, the Commercial Department moved to the Richard Arnold building on Bull Street and became Commercial High School. This photograph shows the school's student council in 1948. The faculty sponsor was Miss Bowe. (Georgia Historical Society, Savannah.)

COMMERCIAL HIGH SCHOOL IN 1950. This 1950 photograph shows Miss Bowe and Commercial High School's student council; this photograph and the one preceding were taken at the building's main entrance. (Georgia Historical Society, Savannah.)

COMMERCIAL HIGH SCHOOL IN 1950. Commercial High School's student council officers were photographed with Miss Bowe, faculty sponsor in 1950. Artie Goodman was the class president. Note the "Commercial Hi" banner on the wall. (Georgia Historical Society, Savannah.)

MISS COMMERCIAL HIGH SCHOOL 1950. Dale Floyd was crowned "Miss Commercial High School" in 1950. Betty Agee, standing at the front left, was first runner-up and Barbara Baker, standing at front right, was second runner-up. They and the other Commercial High beauties posed for this photograph. (Georgia Historical Society, Savannah.)

COMMERCIAL HIGH SCHOOL IN 1950. Commercial High School girls were photographed at the building's main entrance in 1950. The winner and runners-up of the school's beauty pageant have been designated with the appropriate numeral written on their images. (Georgia Historical Society, Savannah.)

LIBRARY NOTICE. Providing on-site library services to the schools' students took considerable time and expense. In the years before schools had their own libraries, Savannah Public Library made its services available—to some students. African-American students were allowed access to facilities run by Chatham County. (Massie Heritage Interpretation Center.)

COMMERCIAL HIGH SCHOOL. Students in this undated photograph study under the watchful eye of their teacher. (Massie Heritage Interpretation Center.)

STUDENT WORK ON DISPLAY. Commercial High School, as its name implied, was a vocational school. This undated photograph shows a display highlighting students' work. (Massie Heritage Interpretation Center.)

SHORTHAND PRACTICE. A student practices her shorthand skills as her teacher looks on. (Massie Heritage Interpretation Center.)

TYPING PRACTICE. Students
work on their typing skills. The
teacher is pointing to a "Typing
Progress Chart." (Massie Heritage
Interpretation Center.)

RADIO BROADCAST. Savannah
High School students produced
live radio broadcasts as early as
the 1930s. In this undated
photograph, African-American
students are participating
in a program broadcast on
radio. (Massie Heritage
Interpretation Center.)

ADDING MACHINES. Commercial High School's future bookkeepers are seen sharpening their skills in this photograph. As ever, the teacher is close at hand. (Massie Heritage Interpretation Center.)

SAVANNAH HIGH SCHOOL SHOP CLASS. A bulletin board in the left background of this photograph identifies the location of this Industrial Arts class as Savannah High School. (Massie Heritage Interpretation Center.)

GRADUATION REHEARSAL. This photograph shows a graduation rehearsal in progress. Dignitaries sit at the table where the diplomas will be handed out, the graduating seniors are center stage, and the school Glee Club rehearses an inspirational song for the commencement exercises. (Massie Heritage Interpretation Center.)

GRADUATION REHEARSAL. A speaker practices his address for the ceremony. (Massie Heritage Interpretation Center.)

GRADUATION REHEARSAL. The candidate practices the receiving of his diploma. (Massie Heritage Interpretation Center.)

THE BIG EVENING. A beaming group of graduates poses for a group photograph. (Massie Heritage Interpretation Center)

ANDERSON STREET SCHOOL. Anderson Street Elementary School students in elaborate costumes pose for a May Day photograph in 1950. (Carolyn Sloop.)

Savannah High School in 1930. Upon graduation, Savannah High School's Class of 1930 traveled to Europe. This album documents their visit to England. Photographs are interspersed with playbills, menus, and postcards. The group sailed for home in RMS *Cedric*. (Massie Heritage Interpretation Center.)

Romana Riley's Grave. Romana Riley died in 1963 and was buried in Bonaventure Cemetery. Her epitaph is from the Old Testament (Daniel 12:3): "And they that be teachers shall shine as the brightness of the firmament." (Photo by the author.)

SAXON P. BARGERON'S GRAVE. Another noteworthy Savannah educator interred in Bonaventure Cemetery is Mrs. Saxon P. Bargeron. Mrs. Bargeron served as a teacher, administrator, superintendent, and president of the school board. Separated by time and distance, Mrs. Bargeron and Emma Truslow had known each other for only a few years when Emma's death ended their dear friendship. Poetically, Emma Truslow (Lipps) is buried a very short distance away from Mrs. Bargeron in an adjoining section of Bonaventure Cemetery. (Photo by the author.)

CHATHAM JUNIOR HIGH BASKETBALL TEAM IN 1962. When Savannah High School relocated to Washington Avenue, its old building at 208 Bull Street was occupied by Chatham Junior High School. Coach Long poses with the Bulldogs basketball team about 1962. Ronnie Smith, #25, and Tonas Goras, #5, were the team's stars. (Wanda Boss.)

Five

RESURRECTION

THE REBIRTH OF DOWNTOWN SCHOOLS

Massie School was closed at the end of the 1973–1974 school year. The building was used as a repository for a time, but citizens and educators organized the "Friends of Massie" committee, and in 1978 Savannah-Chatham County Public Schools reopened it as the Massie Heritage Interpretation Center. Classrooms now house teaching installations and a wide range of programs are available to school groups, civic organizations, and the community. After more than 60 years of service, Savannah High School's Washington Avenue building was closed in favor of a modern new facility on Pennsylvania Avenue. The old building then became Savannah Arts Academy. When Savannah High School first moved from Bull Street to Washington Avenue, "High School" became Chatham Junior High and Oglethorpe Avenue Elementary Schools. Today, the Bull Street facility houses the administrative offices of Savannah-Chatham County Public Schools. The Savannah College of Art and Design has purchased and renovated Anderson Street School, Barnard Street School, 37th Street School, and Henry Street School. Florance Street School, built in 1929, is a beautiful apartment complex today. Charles Herty Elementary School and Richard Arnold Junior High School are also being adapted to residential use. To see the old schools is much akin to time travel. One can easily picture children playing in Massie's "suitable courtyards," or older students walking past Oglethorpe's statue in Chippewa Square as they make their way to class. Savannah's historic public schools are landmarks commemorating the dedication, commitment, and concern of a community for its most important citizens: its young people.

MASSIE FIELD TRIP. Jacob G. Smith Elementary students, with teachers Connie Buckley, Karen Sams, and Heather Lockey, complete a field trip at Massie in 2003. The students visited the *Savannah's Unique City Plan* teaching installation and then went on a walking tour of Savannah's National Landmark Historic District. Back at school, the students wrote essays about their learning experience. (Jacob G. Smith Elementary School.)

BEACH INSTITUTE. The Beach Institute building is today the home of the King-Tisdale Cottage Foundation. The foundation seeks to preserve the cultural history of Savannah's African-American community. (Photo by the author.)

MASSIE DOORS. One of the steps in the process of restoring Massie School was the replacement of its doors with copies of the originals. The new doors are shown in this photograph soon after their installation. (Massie Heritage interpretation Center.)

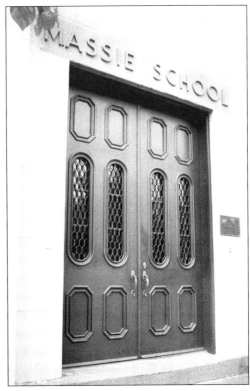

MASSIE CLASSROOM. All third-graders attending Savannah-Chatham County Public Schools have the unique opportunity to visit Massie and participate in the Heritage Classroom program. They experience a school day just as it would have been "in the good old days." Fortunate adults occasionally catch a glimpse of students wearing period dress at work in the old classroom and enjoy a pleasant trip down memory lane. Occasionally, grandparents who attended Massie come to the program with their grandchildren and entertain students with tales of their school days. (Photo by the author.)

ANDERSON STREET SCHOOL. Anderson Street School opened in 1896. The upper-floor hallway had to be partitioned with curtains to create four additional classrooms as soon as it opened because of the rapid growth of its student population. The building is now owned by Savannah College of Art and Design and has been beautifully restored. (Photo by the author.)

ANDERSON STREET SCHOOL. This photograph of the rear of Anderson Street School demonstrates that restoration is a continuous process. Savannahian Ray Nesbitt recalls how, as a mischievous boy, he practiced dropping marbles through a small hole in the lid of a shoebox. The next day during recess at Anderson Street School, he placed a few marbles in the box, demonstrated his prowess at dropping marbles into the box, and challenged his playmates: if they could drop a marble through the hole, they could take a marble out. If they missed, they had to put a marble into the box. His shoebox was soon full of marbles! (Photo by the author.)

BARNARD STREET SCHOOL. Barnard Street School is also owned by Savannah College of Art and Design. In Savannah's National Landmark Historic District, noteworthy architecture is the norm, but the Egyptian revival school building is truly unique. This building opened in 1906. (Photo by the author.)

BARNARD STREET SCHOOL. This view of Barnard Street School shows an addition to the facility. Many of the old schools located library facilities and more classrooms in such additions. (Photo by the author.)

HENRY STREET SCHOOL. In this view of Henry Street School, the outhouses are clearly visible at the left of the photograph. The school opened in 1896. (Photo by the author.)

HENRY STREET SCHOOL. Henry Street School opened in 1892. The building today is home to Savannah College of Art and Design's fashion designing program. (Photo by the author.)

37TH STREET SCHOOL. 37th Street School, an elementary school, opened in 1912. The building now belongs to Savannah College of Art and Design. (Photo by the author.)

37TH STREET SCHOOL. Another view of 37th Street School is shown here. This is one of the most attractive of the restored school buildings. (Photo by the author.)

ROMANA RILEY SCHOOL. Romana Riley School opened as Waters Avenue School in 1915. The school's new name appears over the main entrance. (Photo by the author.)

ROMANA RILEY SCHOOL. Romana Riley School is seen from the rear in this image. This building is used by Savannah-Chatham County Public Schools for administrative office space today. (Photo by the author.)

208 BULL STREET. The facility that once housed Savannah High School, Chatham Junior High School, and Oglethorpe Elementary School today houses the administrative offices of Savannah-Chatham County Public Schools. The print shop is located in the basement, which once accommodated the kitchen and lunchroom. (Photo by the author.)

OGLETHORPE ELEMENTARY SCHOOL. In this photograph, the Chatham Hall-Oglethorpe Elementary School building shows the effects of its age. The plywood sheathing around the top of the building was installed for safety reasons; the masonry façade of the building is crumbling. (Photo by the author.)

PEARL SMITH SCHOOL. Pearl Smith School, named for an African-American pharmacist, opened in 1926. Despite newer additions, some of the original classrooms are in use. The building is home to Oglethorpe Academy today. (Photo by the author.)

PEARL SMITH SCHOOL. This photograph shows an interior view of Pearl Smith School. The room's size reflects thinking on the subject of class size in the early 20th century. (Photo by the author.)

111

PEARL SMITH SCHOOL. Its small size is apparent in this exterior view of Pearl Smith School. Records indicate that the school originally opened in 1926, but it is believed to have opened much earlier. The building's four classrooms originally served about 240 African-American students. (Photo by the author.)

FLORANCE STREET SCHOOL. Florance Street School opened in 1929. It was the first modern elementary school built for the city's African-American children. Because of a stipulation that the William Scarborough House had to be used as a school as long as it was occupied by the school system, Florance Street School complemented West Broad Street Elementary instead of replacing it. A plaque near the entrance honors Miss Emma Quinney, the school's first principal. A remarkable educator, Miss Quinney served her community for more than half a century. (Photo by the author.)

FLORANCE STREET SCHOOL. Florance Street School was restored by the Mercy Housing Division of St. Joseph's/Candler Health System and now provides affordable housing to residents of the Cuyler-Brownville community. The building is a cornerstone of the revitalization of the historic African-American neighborhood. (Photo by the author.)

FLORANCE STREET SCHOOL. Margo King of Mercy Housing's Heritage Place Apartments shows a photographic portrait of Miss Emma Quinney at Florance Street School's main entrance. The portrait was donated by Savannah-Chatham County Public Schools and the Massie Heritage Interpretation Center for display in the building's historical exhibit. After many years away, Miss Quinney has returned to the school she loved so much. (Photo by the author.)

CUYLER STREET SCHOOL. The Cuyler Street School, established in 1913, moved into this building in 1925. Today, it is the home of Savannah's Headstart program. (Photo by the author.)

RICHARD ARNOLD SCHOOL. The Richard Arnold Junior High School building opened in 1921 and was also home to Commercial High School for a number of years. The building is currently being renovated and converted into condominiums. (Photo by the author.)

114

RICHARD ARNOLD SCHOOL. A view of the rear of the Richard Arnold Junior High/Commercial High School building shows how it appears today. Compare this photograph of the rear of the Richard Arnold to the one on page 59. (Photo by the author.)

CHARLES ELLIS SCHOOL. Charles Ellis School opened in 1929 as 48th Street School. It was named after a president of the board of education. The building is now home to Charles Ellis Montessori Academy. (Photo by the author.)

CHARLES ELLIS SCHOOL. A view of the main entrance of the Charles Ellis School building is shown here. (Photo by the author.)

SAVANNAH HIGH SCHOOL. Savannah High School's Washington Avenue facility opened in 1937 and remained in service for six decades. The building also was home to Washington Junior High School for a number of years. The building is the home of Savannah Arts Academy today. (Photo by the author.)

Savannah High School. The Savannah High School building is currently undergoing a renovation. It will continue its service to the community for decades to come. (Photo by the author.)

WILLIAM SCARBOROUGH HOUSE. The William Scarborough House, which served Savannah's African-American children for a century as West Broad Street Elementary School, has been restored to its antebellum splendor. The house is now the home of Ships of the Sea Museum, one of the finest of the many museums located in Savannah's National Landmark Historic District. (Photo by the author.)

OATLAND ISLAND. Oatland Island Education Center is an unusual component of the Savannah-Chatham County Public Schools. The building opened in 1927 as a retirement home for the Brotherhood of Railroad Conductors. During World War II, the building was a Public Health Service hospital; it was then occupied by the Center for Disease Control until 1973. The facility is a center for teaching life sciences and features a nature walk where many species of animal life indigenous to the area can be seen. (Oatland Island Education Center.)

OATLAND ISLAND. A group of students are seen participating in an Oatland program about salt marsh ecosystems. (Oatland Island Education Center.)

OATLAND ISLAND. This photograph shows a group of students setting up camp for an overnight visit to Oatland Island. Massie Heritage Interpretation Center and Oatland Island Education Center offer exceptional out-of-the-classroom learning experiences for the system's students. Savannah-Chatham County Public Schools has been described as "the only school system with its own museum and zoo." Both Massie Heritage Interpretation Center and Oatland Island make their programming and facilities available to the community at large. Both institutions thus have an impact that goes far beyond the students of Savannah-Chatham County Public Schools. (Oatland Island Education Center.)

HERTY SCHOOL. Moore Avenue School, later renamed Charles Herty School, opened in 1942. This building, like Florance Street and Richard Arnold, has been converted to residential use. (Photo by the author.)

HERTY SCHOOL. This photograph shows another view of Charles Herty School. Charles Herty was a research scientist who devoted his career to Georgia's pulp and paper industry.

208 BULL STREET. Savannah High School provides the best illustration of the evolution of Savannah's historic public schools. This building was the school's home until the late 1930s. (Photo by the author.)

500 WASHINGTON AVENUE. This building was Savannah High's home from 1937 until 1997. Washington Junior High School was also housed in this building. (Photo by the author.)

PENNSYLVANIA AVENUE. Savannah High School is located in this modern facility on Pennsylvania Avenue today. (Photo by the author.)

APPENDIX

A Timeline of Savannah-Chatham County
Public Schools, 1788–1982

1788   The Georgia General Assembly mandates the establishment of academies throughout the state; no funds are budgeted for the purpose.

1813   Chatham Academy begins operation. As part of an arrangement with the Union Society, five students are granted scholarships which cover tuition costs.

1841   Peter Massie dies, leaving Savannah the sum of $5,000 "for the education of the children of the poor."

1856   Massie Common School opens. The school is administered by a committee consisting of the city's mayor, three aldermen, and three citizens.

1865   The Savannah Educational Society is organized when Maj. Gen. William T. Sherman occupies Savannah. The society's goal is the education of newly-freed slaves.

1866   The Board of Public Education for Savannah and Chatham County is created.

1866   The Beach Institute is built by the American Missionary Association and the Freedmen's Bureau.

1876   West Broad Street Elementary School opens in the William Scarborough House; it is the first public school for African Americans.

1884   East Broad Street Elementary School opens.

1892   Henry Street School opens.

1895   Maple Street School opens.

1896   Anderson Street School opens.

1899   Chatham Academy's eastern building, fronting Drayton Street, is destroyed in a fire.

1900   38th Street School opens.

1901   Chatham Academy opens a new building, Chatham Hall, to replace the one destroyed in the 1899 fire; demolition begins on the western building.

1905   Chatham Academy opens its new western building. The facility becomes Savannah High School; later, it operates as Chatham Junior High in the western building and Oglethorpe Elementary School in the eastern building.

1906   Barnard Street School opens.

1912   37th Street School opens.

1913   Cuyler School opens.

1915   Waters Avenue School opens. Its name was later changed to Romana Riley Elementary School in honor of one of Savannah's most-loved educators.

1917   Woodville School opens.

1921   Richard Arnold School opens. The building would also serve Commercial High School students in the future.

1926   Pearl Smith School opens.

1929   48th Street School, later Charles Ellis Elementary School, and Florance Street School open.

1936   Tompkins High School opens.

1937   Savannah High School relocates to a new building at 500 Washington Avenue.

1942   Moore Avenue School, later renamed Charles Herty School, opens.

1945   Pennsylvania Avenue Elementary and Port Wentworth Elementary School open.

1949   Pooler Elementary School opens.

1951   Jacob G. Smith Elementary School opens.

1952   Jackson Elementary School opens.

1953   DeRenne Elementary School, Juliette Gordon Low Elementary School, Pulaski Elementary School, Sprague Elementary School, Tompkins Elementary School, and Eli Whitney Elementary School open.

1955   Gadsden Elementary School and Spencer Elementary School open.

1956   Gould Elementary School, Thunderbolt Elementary School, and Tybee Elementary School open.

1957   Jenkins High School, Johnson Elementary School, and White Bluff Elementary School open.

1958   Groves High School opens.

1959   Alfred E. Beach High School, Sol C. Johnson High School, and Wilder Junior High School open.

1960   Myers Junior High School opens.

1962   Bartlett Junior High School, Hubert Junior High School, and Mercer Junior High School open.

1963   Bartow Elementary School, Bloomingdale Elementary School, Butler Elementary School, Scott Junior High School, Strong Elementary, and Shuman High School open.

1964   Windsor Forest Elementary School opens.

1967   Windsor High School opens.

1970   Largo-Tibet Elementary School opens.

1982   East Broad Elementary School moves into a new building.

BIBLIOGRAPHY

Adler, Lee and Emma. *Savannah Renaissance*. Charleston, SC: Wyrick and Co., 2003.

Bargeron, Saxon P. *Historical Sketches of Massie School*. Savannah: Savannah-Chatham County Public Schools, 1980, revised 1997.

Bowden, Haygood S. *Two Hundred Years of Education, 1733–1933, Savannah-Chatham County, Georgia*. Richmond: Dietz Printing Company, 1932.

Brewton, John E., director. *Public Schools in Chatham County, Georgia: A Survey Report*. Nashville: George Peabody College for Teachers, 1949.

Burke, Emily. *Pleasure and Pain*. Savannah: The Beehive Press, 1978.

Coleman, Kenneth, editor. *A History of Georgia*. Athens: UGA Press, 1977.

Riley, Romana. *School Life in Midget Savannah*. Savannah: Commercial Lithograph and Printing Company, 1939.

Thompson, Larry. "Progressive Education in Savannah-Chatham County Schools." Ph.D. diss., University of Georgia, 1986.